CONTENTS

FOREWORD

I usually start a new design by choosing a yarn and color first. I then work with that particular fiber and yarn structure to achieve a fabric that it wants to become. If I try to fight the yarn, the yarn always wins, which is why I love knitting swatches and small accessories to get acquainted with the yarn. For Westknits Book Three, I used a wide variety of yarns from different companies and independent dyers. Some are old favorites while others are new findings.

This collection began in the fall of 2010 with the discovery of a new yarn from Kristen of Skein, an independent hand-dyer in Australia. Her shimmering silk/merino was a dream to knit with and her colors continue to be some of my favorites. The luscious and drapey yarn begged to be around my neck. I listened and made the Moose River cowl, which was the first design for Book Three.

I started with a color palette of steel grays, light blues, greens, and lavender. My Spectra scarf was actually slated to be part of this collection, but I soon found myself gravitating towards my beloved rustic oranges and browns. I'm becoming very predictable when it comes to selecting colors these days. I couldn't force myself to not knit with my favorite natural wools like those from Beaverslide Dry Goods, a family owned and run business in Montana that raises Merino Sheep. Several years ago I made one of Elizabeth Zimmermann's Pi Shawls and loved the process of knitting the large round fabric. I've always wanted to make another circular blanket, so I utilized the soft Beaverslide yarn to create Old Forge.

MOOSE RIVER

OLD FORGE

4

Another favorite wool of mine is Elsa Wool, a ranch in southwestern Colorado, that raises Cormo sheep. This incredibly soft sheep breed produces the most comforting fabric, which I used for the slouchy textured Dustland Hat.

I knit another Dustland Hat using Swans Island 100% organic merino yarn from Maine to add some light natural color to the book's palette. You won't believe how soft and drapey this yarn becomes, especially after blocking.

One of my trips to London's Loop yarn shop brought me in contact with Shilasdair, a company in Scotland that uses natural dyes to achieve stunning effects. I promptly whipped up a pair of slouchy fingerless mitts in an Angora/Cashmere/Lambswool blend to match the Dustland Hat.

DUSTLAND HAT

WEDGEWOOD

DUSTLAND MITTS

I continue my love of mixing natural colors with hand-dyed yarns in the Wedgewood Scarf. Another favorite hand-dyer of mine, Beata from Ireland, never ceases to amaze me with her range of subtle to intense colorways that she dyes under the name Hedgehog Fibres. I combined Beata's yak/bamboo blend with her variegated sock yarn in this lengthwise scarf with buttons.

Continued...

LONGVIEW

Misti Alpaca, based in Illinois, gets its alpaca from Peru and they do a nice hand-dyed alpaca/merino blend featured in the Longview scarf and cowl. The alpaca gives the fabric a nice density and drape while the merino wool provides brilliant body and stitch definition, perfect for seed stitch and thick cables.

Madelinetosh is always a go-to yarn for me when knitting a design with more than one color. Their color range is phenomenal and the iridescent Pashmina yarn base makes simple colorwork and stitch patterns shine. The cashmere content doesn't hurt either. Semi-solid colorways like Boxwood and Wren highlight and shade the fabric making us knitters look very clever and classy. I returned to one of my favorite shawl shapes, same shape as Herbivore, because I find myself wearing that shape the most as a casual everyday scarf. Thendara is essentially a striped Herbivore with a different stitch pattern in the increase motifs: simple, fun, and striking!

THENDARA

SEAWAY

BEDROCK

SUN SATCHEL

My red Sundara Windschief hat is my all-time favorite hat to wear so I tried to make another favorite grab-and-go hat, which resulted in Seaway, a beanie with cables and twisted stitches. I returned to the Windschief construction method because a quarter of the fabric is worked on a bias, giving the brim an asymmetric angle that frames the face nicely. I love this shape for a men's hat, but it looks just as good on women too. This time I chose a lighter DK weight fabric with Rowan Felted Tweed. I've been grabbing this hat all the time.

I've seen The Fibre Company yarns in local shops before, but never knit with them until recently when I used Road to China Light for my first Mystery Shawl KAL. That yarn is pure luxury and Terra doesn't disappoint either. The sophisticated

colors in addition to Terra's heavenly soft and rustic texture make it a stand-out yarn. I haven't seen anything like it before and I only used two skeins to make Bedrock, a bumpy textured hat that can be slouchy or more fitted if you fold the asymmetric brim. The dense alpaca makes it one of my coziest hats to date.

One of the last additions to the collection was the Sun Satchel using Noro Kureyon and a local wool produced in Portugal called Retrosaria Beiroa. I went through a big felting phase about 4 years ago and remembered why I felted so much after making this bag. The felting transformation is always a magical experience when you pull your new woolen creation out of the washing machine. It's suddenly not so magical when you pull out a sweater that was accidentally thrown in the wash.

I adore discovering new yarns to play with, and I'm always comforted by my favorites that I return to time and time again. I hope you will enjoy knitting these designs with your own favorite yarns or you can try using some of the ones I recommended. Either way, I hope you find some inspiration within these pages as you knit for yourself and others .

Stephen

LONGVIEW

Longview is a chunky textural scarf with exaggerated cables and seed stitch. Knit the larger dramatic scarf or follow instructions for a smaller neckwarmer. The neckwarmer features a hole in the fabric and a button closure so that one end can enter into the hole and wrap around the neck to be buttoned. Choosing a soft chunky yarn will make this project both quick and enjoyable.

Sizes: Neckwarmer [Scarf]
Finished Measurements: 7" / 18cm wide, 42 [84]" / 107 [213]cm long.
Yarn: Chunky weight
Yardage: Neckwarmer - 215yds / 197m, Scarf – 465yds / 425m
Shown in: Misti Alpaca Tonos Chunky (50% Baby Alpaca, 50% Merino; 109yds / 100m per 100g skein), Colorway: (Neckwarmer) Avocado, (Scarf) Nazca
Needles: US 10 / 6mm straight
Notions: Cable needle, 2 stitch markers, tapestry needle, 1.5" button for neckwarmer
Gauge: 14 sts and 20 rows = 4" / 10cm in seed stitch

Pattern Notes: Sections 1 & 2 each use approximately 32yds / 29m.

Reading the Charts: Sections 1, 2 & 3 are charted, but also refer to written instructions for scarf or neckwarmer instructions. Charts are read from right to left on odd numbered rows and from left to right on even numbered rows.

INSTRUCTIONS

NECKWARMER

CO 3 sts.

*K3. Do not turn to work other side, slip 3 sts back to left needle, repeat from * until I-cord measures approximately 3" / 8cm. Turn to work next WS row.

Set Up Row (WS): Pfb, p2. 4 sts.

Continue to SECTION 1 using written or charted instructions.

SCARF

CO 4 sts.

Set Up Row (WS): P4.

Continue by following SECTION 1 using written or charted instructions.

SECTION 1

Row 1 (RS): K1, M1L, p1, k2. 5 sts.
Row 2 (WS): P2, k1, p2.
Row 3 (RS): K1, M1L, k1, p1, k1, M1L, k1. 7 sts.
Row 4 (WS): P3, k1, p3.
Row 5 (RS): K1, M1L, k2, p1, k1, M1L, k2. 9 sts.
Row 6 (WS): P4, k1, p4.
Row 7 (RS): K4, p1, k4.
Row 8 (WS): P4, k1, p4.
Row 9 (RS): C4B, p1, C4F.
Row 10 (WS): P4, k1, p4.
Row 11 (RS): K1, M1L, k3, p1, k1, M1L, k3. 11 sts.

Row 12 (WS): P5, k1, p5.
Row 13 (RS): K1, M1L, k4, p1, k1, M1L, k4. 13 sts.
Row 14 (WS): P6, k1, p6.
Row 15 (RS): C6B, p1, C6F.
Row 16 (WS): P6, k1, p6.
Row 17 (RS): K1, M1L, k5, p1, k1, M1L, k5. 15 sts.
Row 18 (WS): P7, k1, p7.
Row 19 (RS): K1, M1L, k6, p1, k1, M1L, k6. 17 sts.
Row 20 (WS): P8, k1, p8.
Row 21 (RS): K1, M1L, k1, C6B, p1, C6F, k1, M1L, k1. 19 sts.
Row 22 (WS): P9, k1, p9.
Row 23 (RS): K1, M1L, k8, p1, k1, M1L, k8. 21 sts.
Row 24 (WS): P10, k1, p10.

SECTION 1

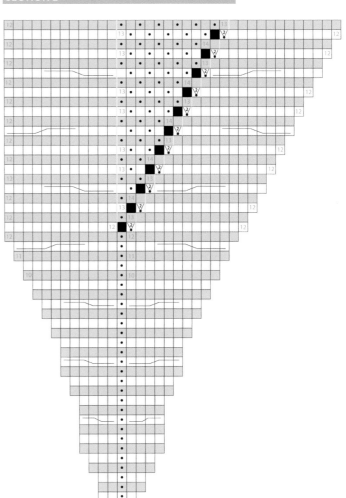

	No Stitch		Purl into front and back of stitch
	C2B		P2tog
	C2F		P3tog
	Kfb	•	Purl on the RS, Knit on the WS
	C8F		Knit on the RS, Purl on the WS
	C8B		K2tog
	C6B		SSK
	C6F		M1L
	C4B		Place or slip marker
	C4F		

Numbers in blue text indicate the number of plain stitches that are worked in longer stretches of the chart so that you don't have to count the number of boxes!

Row 25 (RS): K1, M1L, k9, p1, k1, M1L, k9. 23 sts.

Row 26 (WS): P11, k1, p11.

Row 27 (RS): C8F, k2, M1L, k1, p1, k1, M1L, k2, C8B. 25 sts.

Row 28 (WS): P12, k1, p12.

It may help to place a stitch marker after the first 12 sts and before the last 12 sts.

Row 29 (RS): K12, pfb, k12. 26 sts.

Row 30 (WS): P12, k1, p13.

Row 31 (RS): K12, pfb, k13. 27 sts.

Row 32 (WS): P12, k1, p14.

Row 33 (RS): K4, C8B, pfb, p1, k1, C8F, k4. 28 sts.

Row 34 (WS): P12, (k1, p1) twice, p12.

Row 35 (RS): K12, pfb, k1, p1, k13. 29 sts.

Row 36 (WS): P12, (k1, p1) twice, p13.

Row 37 (RS): K12, pfb, (p1, k1) twice, k12. 30 sts.

Row 38 (WS): P12, (k1, p1) 3 times, p12.

Row 39 (RS): C8F, k4, pfb, (k1, p1) twice, k5, C8B. 31 sts.

Row 40 (WS): P12, (k1, p1) 3 times, p13.

Row 41 (RS): K12, pfb, (p1, k1) 3 times k12. 32 sts.

Row 42 (WS): P12, (k1, p1) 4 times, p12.

Row 43 (RS): K12, pfb, (k1, p1) 3 times, k13. 33 sts.

Row 44 (WS): P12, (k1, p1) 4 times, p13.

Row 45 (RS): K4, C8B, pfb, (p1, k1) 4 times, C8F, k4. 34 sts.

Row 46 (WS): P12, (k1, p1) 5 times. p12.

Row 47 (RS): K12, pfb, (k1, p1) 4 times, k13. 35 sts.

Row 48 (WS): P12, (k1, p1) 5 times, p13.

Row 49 (RS): K12, pfb, (p1, k1) 5 times, k12. 36 sts.

Row 50 (WS): P12, (k1, p1) 6 times, p12.

SECTION 2

Row 1 (RS): C8F, k4, (p1, k1) 6 times, k4, C8B.

All WS rows: P12, (k1, p1) 6 times, p12.

Row 3 (RS): K12, (p1, k1) 6 times, k12.

Row 5 (RS): K12, (p1, k1) 6 times, k12.

Row 7 (RS): K4, C8B, (p1, k1) 6 times, C8F, k4.

Row 9 (RS): K12, (p1, k1) 6 times, k12.

Row 11 (RS): K12, (p1, k1) 6 times, k12.

Row 12 (WS): P12, (k1, p1) 6 times, p12.

Repeat last 12 rows 14 [33] more times or until

SECTION 3

Legend:

- ■ No Stitch
- C2B
- C2F
- Kfb
- C8F
- C8B
- C6B
- C6F
- C4B
- C4F
- Purl into front and back of stitch
- P2tog
- P3tog
- • Purl on the RS, Knit on the WS
- □ Knit on the RS, Purl on the WS
- K2tog
- SSK
- M1L
- Place or slip marker
- Numbers in blue text indicate the number of plain stitches that are worked in longer stretches of the chart so that you don't have to count the number of boxes!

SECTION 2

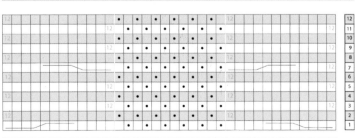

work measures approximately 32 [72]" / 81 [183] cm from CO edge, ending with Row 12 (WS). Continue by following NECKWARMER or SCARF instructions.

NECKWARMER

Next Row (One Row Buttonhole): C8F, k4, sl1 wyif, (sl1 wyib, pass first slipped stitch over second) 12 times, place last st back onto left-hand needle. Turn to work on the WS. (Insert right needle between the first and second st on the left-hand needle, wrap strand of yarn around right needle as you would for a knit stitch and pull through, place that loop onto left-hand needle) 13 times. Turn to work on the RS. Wyib sl first st of left-hand needle onto right-hand needle, pass last CO st over it, k3, C8B.

Next Row (WS): P12, (k1, p1) 6 times, p12.

Continue to SECTION 3

SCARF

Repeat Rows 1 & 2 once more and continue to SECTION 3.

SECTION 3

Row 1 (RS): K12, p2tog, (p1, k1) 5 times, k12. 35 sts.

Row 2 (WS): P12, (k1, p1) 5 times, p13.

Row 3 (RS): K12, p2tog, (k1, p1) 4 times, k13. 34 sts.

Row 4 (WS): P12, (k1, p1) 5 times. p12.

Row 5 (RS): K4, C8B, p2tog, (p1, k1) 4 times, C8F, k4. 33 sts.

Row 6 (WS): P12, (k1, p1) 4 times, p13.

Row 7 (RS): K12, p2tog, (k1, p1) 3 times, k13. 32 sts.

Row 8 (WS): P12, (k1, p1) 4 times, p12.

Row 9 (RS): K12, p2tog, (p1, k1) 3 times k12. 31 sts.

Row 10 (WS): P12, (k1, p1) 3 times, p13.

Row 11 (RS): C8F, k4, p2tog, (k1, p1) twice, k5, C8B. 30 sts.

Row 12 (WS): P12, (k1, p1) 3 times, p12.

Row 13 (RS): K12, p2tog, (k1, p1) twice, k12. 29 sts.

Row 14 (WS): P12, (k1, p1) twice, p13.

Row 15 (RS): K12, p2tog, k1, p1, k13. 28 sts.

Row 16 (WS): P12, (k1, p1) twice, p12.

Row 17 (RS): K4, C8B, p2tog, p1, k1, C8F, k4. 27 sts.

Row 18 (WS): P12, k1, p14.

Row 19 (RS): K12, p2tog, k13. 26 sts.

Row 20 (WS): P12, k1, p13.

Row 21 (RS): K12, p2tog, k12. 25 sts.

Row 22 (WS): P12, k1, p12.

Row 23 (RS): C8F, k1, ssk, k1, p1, k1, ssk, k1, C8B. 23 sts.

Row 24 (WS): P11, k1, p11.

Row 25 (RS): K1, ssk, k8, p1, k1, ssk, k8. 21 sts.

Row 26 (WS): P10, k1, p10.

Row 27 (RS): K1, ssk, k7, p1, k1, ssk, k7. 19 sts.

Row 28 (WS): P9, k1, p9.

Row 29 (RS): K1, ssk, C6B, p1, C6F, ssk, k1. 17 sts.

Row 30 (WS): P8, k1, p8.

Row 31 (RS): K1, ssk, k5, p1, k1, ssk, k5. 15 sts.

Row 32 (WS): P7, k1, p7.

Row 33 (RS): K1, ssk, k4, p1, k1, ssk, k4. 13 sts.

Row 34 (WS): P6, k1, p6.

Row 35 (RS): C6B, p1, C6F.

Row 36 (WS): P6, k1, p6.

Row 37 (RS): K1, ssk, k3, p1, k1, ssk, k3. 11 sts.

Row 38 (WS): P5, k1, p5.

Row 39 (RS): K1, ssk, k2, p1, k1, ssk, k2. 9 sts.

Row 40 (WS): P4, k1, p4.

Row 41 (RS): C4B, p1, C4F.

Row 42 (WS): P4, k1, p4.

Row 43 (RS): K4, p1, k4.

Row 44 (WS): P4, k1, p4.

Row 45 (RS): K1, ssk, k1, p1, k1, ssk, k1. 7 sts.

Row 46 (WS): P3, k1, p3.

Row 47 (RS): K1, ssk, p1, k1, ssk. 5 sts.

Row 48 (WS): P2, k1, p2.

Row 49 (RS): Ssk, p1, ssk. 3 sts.

Row 50 (WS): P3tog.

FINISHING

Break yarn and pull it through last remaining stitch. Sew I-cord closed to form a buttonhole on the neckwarmer. Then, sew a button at the other end as pictured. Weave in ends.

SUN SATCHEL

This circular bag is a fun adventure in felting and simple colorwork. Two circles are worked outward from the center to create a graphic sun motif. Then, the sides of the bag and strap are knit in one continuous piece and seamed to the two sun circles before felting. Optional afterthought pockets store belongings inside the bag while a button and loop secure the top flap for a semi-circular look.

Finished Measurements: 22" / 56cm diameter before blocking. 16" / 41cm diameter after blocking. The size of the finished bag can vary depending on how severely it is blocked.
Yarn: Worsted weight
Shown in: Retrosaria Beiroa (100% Wool; 273yds / 250m per 100g skein), Colorway: Natural
Noro Kureyon (100% Wool; 110yds / 101m per 50g skein), Colorway: 149
Yardage: Color A – 375yds / 343m (includes optional pockets)
Color B – 620yds / 567m
Needles: 1 set US 9 / 5.5mm DPNS
32" US 9 / 5.5mm circular
9/I / 5.5mm crochet hook for CO
Notions: Tapestry needle, 1.5" / 4cm button
Gauge: 16 sts and 28 rows = 4" / 10 cm in garter stitch

Pattern Notes: Stitches are slipped wyib. m1: (make one) increase one stitch by knitting into the stitch below

INSTRUCTIONS

FRONT & BACK

Using color A and DPNs, CO 8 sts. I used Emily Ocker's circular CO method. Distribute sts evenly onto 4 DPNs. Place marker and join to work in the rnd. Switch to circular needles when there are too many sts to fit onto DPNs.

Rnd 1: K8.

Rnd 2: (M1, k1) 8 times. 16 sts.

Rnd 3: K16.

Rnd 4: (M1, k1) 16 times. 32 sts.

Next 4 rnds: K all sts.

Rnd 9: (M1, k1) 32 times. 64 sts.

Next 10 rnds: K all sts.

Rnd 20: (M1, k1) 64 times. 128 sts.

SECTION 2

Rnds 1 & 2: Using color A, k all sts.

Rnd 3: Using color B, (k6, sl2) 16 times.

Rnd 4: (P6, sl2) 16 times.

Repeat last 4 rnds 5 more times.

Rnd 25: Using color A, k all sts.

Rnd 26: *(M1, k1) 6 times, k2, repeat from * 15 more times. 224 sts.

Rnd 27: Using color B, (k12, sl2) 16 times.

Rnd 28: (P12, sl2) 16 times.

Rnds 29 & 30: Using color A, k all sts.

Rnd 31: Using color B, (k12, sl2) 16 times.

Rnd 32: (P12, sl2) 16 times.

Rnds 33 & 34: Using color A, k all sts.

Rnd 35: Using color B, (k26, sl2) 8 times.

Rnd 36: (P26, sl2) 8 times.

Repeat last 4 rnds 7 more times.

Rnd 65 & 66: Using color A, k all sts.

Rnd 67: Using color B, k all sts.

Rnd 68: P all sts.

BO all sts on following rnd. Repeat instructions again to make an identical circle for the bag's other side.

EDGE & STRAP

Using color B, CO 24 sts.

K 276 rows (138 garter ridges).

Next Row (RS): K1, ssk, k to last 3 sts, k2tog, k1.
Next 3 Rows: K all sts.

Repeat last 4 rows 5 more times. 12 sts remain.

K 248 rows (124 garter ridges).

Next Row (RS): Kfb, k to last 2 sts, kfb, k1.
Next 3 Rows: K all sts.

Repeat last 4 rows 5 more times. 24 sts remain. BO all sts. Sew together BO and CO edges.

POCKETS (OPTIONAL)

Small Pocket (ideal for cell phone, pens, or a little snack)

Using color A, CO 20 sts.

K 56 rows (28 garter ridges).

Sew pocket to inside of the side strap.

Large Pocket (ideal for wallet, camera, or a bigger snack)

Using color A, CO 32 sts.

K 56 rows (28 garter ridges).

Sew pocket to inside of sun motif.

FINISHING

To assemble the bag, sew the side edge piece (the part that is 24 sts wide) to the sun motif circles as pictured using color B. The thin strap and increase section of the strap is not sewn to the sun circles, only the 24-stitch wide strip of fabric is attached to the sun circles. Felting will help hide any untidy sewing.

I-cord buttonhole: Using color A, CO 3 sts. *K3, sl those 3 sts back to left needle, repeat from * until I-cord measures approximately 5" / 13cm. Break yarn and pull it through the 3 sts. Sew I-cord to top edge of sun circle as pictured.

Weave in ends. Felt the bag by putting it into the washing machine on a hot wash cycle, checking regularly on its progress. Sew button to the center of the sun motif that doesn't have the buttonhole so it can close as pictured.

MOOSE RIVER

Wrap yourself in luxury with this slouchy cowl. Reversible cables and simple knit purl stitch patterns saturate the fabric with texture, resulting in a completely reversible design. I chose a delicious silk/merino single ply for a drapey effect, but alpaca or wool yarns would also make wonderful fabrics.

Finished Measurements: 14" / 36cm long from CO to BO, 36" / 91cm circumference
Yarn: Worsted weight
Yardage: 600yds / 549m
Shown in: Skein Merino/Silk Worsted (50% Merino, 50% Silk; 165yds / 151m per 100g skein), Colorway: Industrial Age
Needles: 24" US 8 / 5mm circular
Notions: 1 stitch marker, cable needle, tapestry needle
Gauge: 24 sts and 24 rows = 4" / 10cm in 1x1 ribbing (unstretched)

Reading the Chart: All chart rnds are read from right to left starting at the bottom.

INSTRUCTIONS

CO 117 sts using a tubular CO and work tubular CO or CO 234 sts using a regular cast on. Place marker and join to work in the rnd, being careful not to twist sts. Continue by following written or charted instructions.

(P1, k1) to end of rnd.

Repeat last rnd until work measures approximately 2.5" / 6.5cm from CO edge.

Next 2 rnds: *(K1, p1) twice, (p1, k1) twice, k1, (p4, k4) 3 times, p4, k2, p1 (k1, p1) 3 times, (p1, k1) 6 times, k8, (p1, k1) 6 times, repeat from * 2 more times.

Rnd 1: *(P1, k1) 3 times, p1, (C4F, C4B) 4 times, p1, k1, p1, (p1, k1) twice, C12B, p8, C12F, repeat from * 2 more times.

Rnd 2: *(P1, k1) 3 times, p3, (k4, p4) 3 times, k4, p3, k1, p1, (p1, k1) 8 times, p8, (p1, k1) 6 times, repeat from * 2 more times.

Rnds 3 & 4: *(K1, p1) twice, p1, k1, p3, (k4, p4) 3 times, k4, p3, (k1, p1) 3 times, (p1, k1) 6 times, k8, (p1, k1) 6 times, repeat from * 2 more times.

Rnd 5: *(P1, k1) 3 times, p1, (C4B, C4F) 4 times, p1, k1, p1, (p1, k1) 8 times, p8, (p1, k1) 6 times, repeat from * 2 more times.

Rnd 6: : *(P1, k1) 3 times, p1, k2, (p4, k4) 3 times, p4, k2, p1, k1, p1, (p1, k1) 8 times, p8, (p1, k1) 6 times, repeat from * 2 more times.

Rnds 7 & 8: *(K1, p1) twice, (p1, k1) twice, k1, (p4, k4) 3 times, p4, k2, (p1, k1) 3 times, p1, (p1, k1) 6 times, k8, (p1, k1) 6 times.

Repeat last 8 rnds 7 more times or until work measures approximately 11.5" / 29cm. Repeat rnds 1 & 2 once more.

Next Rnd: (P1, k1) to end of rnd.

Repeat last rnd until work 1x1 ribbing measures approximately 2.5" / 6.5cm.

FINISHING

BO all sts using a tubular BO or your preferred BO. Break yarn and weave in ends.

	C12F
	C12B
	C4B
	C4F
•	Purl
	Knit
|	Repeat Section

Numbers in blue text indicate the number of plain stitches that are worked in longer stretches of the chart so that you don't have to count the number of boxes!

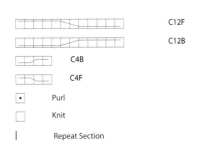

SEAWAY

This stylish beanie hugs the head with its soft and tweedy fabric. A quarter of the hat features twisted stitches and cables worked on a bias. This biased section also gives the brim a slight asymmetric angle that frames the face with subtle fierceness.

Finished Measurements: 21" / 53cm circumference. Hat is designed to fit an average 21" / 53cm to 24" / 61cm circumference head. Hat is shown on a 22.5" / 57cm head. Different sizes can easily be achieved by altering needle size and/or yarn weight.

Yarn: DK weight

Yardage: 140yds / 128m

Shown in: Rowan Felted Tweed (50% Merino, 25% Alpaca, 25% Viscose; 191yds / 175m per 50g skein), Colorway: (Orange) 154 Ginger

Notions: 1 stitch marker, tapestry needle

Gauge: 24 sts and 32 rows = 4" / 10cm in stockinette stitch using US 3 / 3.25mm needles

Needles: 16" US 2 / 2.75mm
16" US 3 / 3.25mm
1 set US 3 / 3.25mm DPNs

INSTRUCTIONS

Using US 2 / 2.75mm needles, CO 120 sts. Place marker and join to work in the rnd, being careful not to twist sts.

Twisted Rib Brim: (p1, k1tbl) to end of rnd.

Repeat Twisted Rib until work measures 1.5" / 4cm from CO edge.

Set Up Rnd 1: Using US 3 / 3.25mm needles, p1, k89, pm, *p1, k1tbl, (p1, M1L) 3 times, k1tbl, (M1L, p1) 3 times, k1tbl*, p1, (p1, M1L) twice, p1, (k1, M1L) 3 times, (p1, M1L) twice p1, repeat from * to * once. 139 sts.

Set Up Rnd 2: P1, k to m, slm, p1, k1tbl, (p6, k1tbl) twice, p6, k6, (p6, k1tbl) 3 times.

Rnd 1: P1, k1, M1L, k to 2 sts before m, k2tog, slm, p1, k1tbl, p4, C2B, k1tbl, C2F, p4, k1tbl, p4, C2B, C6B, C2F, p4, k1tbl, p4, C2B, k1tbl, C2F, p4, k1tbl.

Rnd 2: P1, k to m, slm, p1, k1tbl, p4, (k1tbl, p1) twice, (k1tbl, p4) twice, k1tbl, p1, k6, p1, k1tbl, (p4, k1tbl) twice, (p1, k1tbl) twice, p4, k1tbl.

Rnd 3: P1, k1, M1L, k to 2 sts before m, k2tog, slm, p1, k1tbl, p3, C2B, p1, k1tbl, p1, C2F, p3, k1tbl, p3, C2B, p1, k6, p1, C2F, p3, k1tbl, p3, C2B, p1, k1tbl, p1, C2F, p3, k1tbl.

Rnd 4: P1, k to m, slm, p1, k1tbl, p3, (k1tbl, p2) twice, (k1tbl, p3) twice, k1tbl, p2, k6, p2, (k1tbl, p3) twice, (p2, k1tbl) twice, p3, k1tbl.

Rnd 5: P1, k1, M1L, k to 2 sts before m, k2tog, slm, p1, k1tbl, p2, C2B, p2, k1tbl, p2, C2F, p2, k1tbl, p2, C2B, p2, C6B, p2, C2F, p2, k1tbl, p2, C2B, p2, k1tbl, p2, C2F, p2, k1tbl.

Rnd 6: P1, k to m, slm, p1, k1tbl, p2, (k1tbl, p3) twice, (k1tbl, p2) twice, k1tbl, p3, k6, p3, (p2, k1tbl) twice, (p3, k1tbl) twice, p2, k1tbl.

Rnd 7: P1, k1, M1L, k to 2 sts before m, k2tog, slm, p1, k1tbl, p1, C2B, p3, k1tbl, p3, C2F, p1, k1tbl, p1, C2B, p3, k6, p3, C2F, p1, k1tbl, p1, C2B, p3, k1tbl, p3, C2F, p1, k1tbl.

Rnd 8: P1, k to m, slm, (p1, k1tbl) twice, (p1, k1tbl) twice, (p4, k1tbl) twice, p4, k6, p4, (p1, k1tbl) twice, (k1tbl, p4) twice, k1tbl, p1, k1tbl.

Rnd 9: P1, k1, M1L, k to 2 sts before m, k2tog, slm, p1, k1tbl, p4, C2B, k1tbl, C2F, p4, k1tbl, p1, C2F, p3, C6B, p3, C2B, p1, k1tbl, p4, C2B, k1tbl, C2F, p4, k1tbl.

Rnd 10: P1, k to m, slm, p1, k1tbl, p4, k1tbl, (p1, k1tbl) twice, p4, k1tbl, p2, k1tbl, p3, k6, p3, k1tbl, p2, k1tbl, p4, (k1tbl, p1) twice, k1tbl, p4, k1tbl.

Rnd 11: P1, k1, M1L, k to 2 sts before m, k2tog, slm, p1, k1tbl, p3, C2B, p1, k1tbl, p1, C2F, p3, k1tbl, p2, C2F, p2, k6, p2, C2B, p2, k1tbl, p3, C2B, p1, k1tbl, p1, C2F, p3, k1tbl.

Rnd 12: P1, k to m, slm, p1, k1tbl, p3, k1tbl, p2, k1tbl, p2, k1tbl, p3, k1tbl, p3, k1tbl, p2, k6, p2, p3, k1tbl, p3, k1tbl, p2, k1tbl, p2, k1tbl, p3, k1tbl.

Rnd 13: P1, k1, M1L, k to 2 sts before m, k2tog, slm, p1, k1tbl, p2, C2B, p2, k1tbl, p2, C2F, p2, k1tbl, p3, C2F, p1, C6B, p1, C2B, p3, k1tbl, p2, C2B, p2, k1tbl, p2, C2F, p2, k1tbl.

Rnd 14: P1, k to m, slm, p1, k1tbl, p2, k1tbl, p3, k1tbl, p3, k1tbl, p2, k1tbl, p4, k1tbl, p1, k6, p1, k1tbl, p4, k1tbl, p2, k1tbl, p3, k1tbl, p3, k1tbl, p2, k1tbl.

Rnd 15: P1, k1, M1L, k to 2 sts before m, k2tog, slm, p1, k1tbl, p1, C2B, p3, k1tbl, p3, C2F, p1, k1tbl, p4, C2F, k6, C2B, p4, k1tbl, p1, C2B, p3, k1tbl, p3, C2F, p1, k1tbl.

Rnd 16: P1, k to m, slm, (p1, k1tbl) twice, (p4, k1tbl) twice, p1, k1tbl, p5, k1tbl, k6, k1tbl, p5, k1tbl, p1, (k1tbl, p4) twice, k1tbl, p1, k1tbl.

Repeat last 16 rnds once more, ending with Rnd 16. Work should measure approximately 5.5" / 14cm from CO edge. Switch to DPNs when there are not enough sts to work on circular needles.

CROWN SHAPING

Rnd 33: P1, k25, k2tog twice, (k26, k2tog twice) twice, slm, p1, k1tbl, p4, C2B, k1tbl, C2F, p4, k1tbl, p4, C2B, C6B, C2F, p4, k1tbl, p4, C2B, k1tbl, p1, k2tog 3 times. 130 sts.

Rnd 34: P1, k to m, slm, p1, k1tbl, p4, (k1tbl, p1) twice, (k1tbl, p4) twice, k1tbl, p1, k6, p1, k1tbl, (p4, k1tbl) twice, p1, k1tbl, p1, k3.

Rnd 35: P1, k23, k2tog twice, (k24, k2tog twice) twice, slm, p1, k1tbl, p3, C2B, p1, k1tbl, p1, C2F, p3, k1tbl, p3, C2B, p1, k6, p1, C2F, p3, k1tbl, p3, C2B, k2tog 3 times. 121 sts.

Rnd 36: P1, k to m, slm, p1, k1tbl, p3, (k1tbl, p2) twice, (k1tbl, p3) twice, k1tbl, p2, k6, p2, k1tbl, (p3, k1tbl) twice, p1, k3.

Rnd 37: P1, k21, k2tog twice, (k22, k2tog twice) twice, slm, p1, k1tbl, p2, C2B, p2, k1tbl, p2, C2F, p2, k1tbl, p2, C2B, p2, C6B, p2, C2F, p2, k1tbl, p2, k2tog 3 times. 112 sts.

Rnd 38: P1, k to m, slm, p1, k1tbl, p2, (k1tbl, p3) twice, (k1tbl, p2) twice, k1tbl, p3, k6, p3, k1tbl, p2, k1tbl, p2, k3.

Rnd 39: P1, k19, k2tog twice, (k20, k2tog twice) twice, slm, p1, k1tbl, p1, C2B, p3, k1tbl, p3, C2F, p1, k1tbl, p1, C2B, p3, k6, p3, C2F, p1, k2tog 3 times. 103 sts.

Rnd 40: P1, k to m, slm, (p1, k1tbl) twice, (p4, k1tbl) twice, (p1, k1tbl) twice, p4, k6, p4, k1tbl, p1, k3.

Rnd 41: P1, k17, k2tog twice, (k18, k2tog twice) twice, slm, p1, k1tbl, p4, C2B, k1tbl, C2F, p4, k1tbl, p1, C2F, p3, C6B, p3, k2tog 3 times. 94 sts.

Rnd 42: P1, k to m, slm, p1, k1tbl, p4, k1tbl, (p1, k1tbl) twice, p4, k1tbl, p2, k1tbl, p3, k6, p3, k3.

Rnd 43: P1, k15, k2tog twice, (k16, k2tog twice) twice, slm, p1, k1tbl, p3, C2B, p1, k1tbl, p1, C2F, p3, k1tbl, p2, C2F, p2, k6, k2tog 3 times. 85 sts.

Rnd 44: P1, k to m, slm, p1, k1tbl, p3, k1tbl, p2, k1tbl, p2, k1tbl, p3, k1tbl, p3, k1tbl, p2, k9.

Rnd 45: P1, k13, k2tog twice, (k14, k2tog twice) twice, slm, p1, k1tbl, p2, C2B, p2, k1tbl, p2, C2F, p2, k1tbl, p3, C2F, p1, k3, k2tog 3 times. 76 sts.

Rnd 46: P1, k to m, slm, p1, k1tbl, p2, k1tbl, p3, k1tbl, p3, k1tbl, p2, k1tbl, p4, k1tbl, p1, k6.

Rnd 47: P1, k11, k2tog twice, (k12, k2tog twice) twice, slm, p1, k1tbl, p1, C2B, p3, k1tbl, p3, C2F, p1, k1tbl, p4, C2F, k2tog 3 times. 67 sts.

Rnd 48: P1, k to m, slm, (p1, k1tbl) twice, (p4, k1tbl) twice, p1, k1tbl, p5, k1tbl, k3.

Rnd 49: P1, k9, k2tog twice, (k10, k2tog twice) twice, slm, p1, k1tbl, p4, C2B, k1tbl, C2F, p4, k1tbl, p3, k2tog 3 times. 58 sts.

Rnd 50: P1, k7, k2tog twice, (k8, k2tog twice) twice, slm, p1, k1tbl, p4, (k1tbl, p1) twice, k1tbl, p3, k2tog 4 times. 48 sts.

Rnd 51: P1, k5, k2tog twice, (k6, k2tog twice) twice, slm, p1, k1tbl, p3, C2B, p1, k1tbl, p1, k2tog 4 times. 38 sts.

Rnd 52: P1, k3, k2tog twice, (k4, k2tog twice) twice, slm, p1, k1tbl, p3, k1tbl, k2tog 4 times. 28 sts.

Rnd 53: P1, k1, k2tog twice, (k2, k2tog twice) twice, slm, p1, k1tbl, k2tog 4 times. 18 sts.

Rnd 54: K2tog 9 times. 9 sts.

FINISHING

Break yarn and pull strand through remaining 9 sts. Weave in ends and block hat.

BEDROCK

I love playing with different brim shapes! This hat uses short row shaping to create a wider section so that the brim can be folded up, giving your noggin extra warmth and an asymmetrical accent. The brim can also be worn unfolded and pushed back for a slouchy effect. Loose bobble stitch gives a density and textural interest to the main body of the hat.

Finished Measurements: 21" / 53cm brim circumference, Hat is designed to fit an average 21" / 53cm to 24" / 61cm circumference head. Hat is shown on a 22.5" / 57cm head. Different sizes can easily be achieved by altering needle size and/or yarn weight.
Yarn: Worsted weight
Yardage: 196yds / 179m
Shown in: The Fibre Company Terra (40% Baby Alpaca, 40% Wool, 20% Silk; 98yds / 90m per 50g skein), Colorway: Black Walnut
Needles: 16" US 7 / 4.5mm circular
1 set US 7 / 4.5mm DPNs
Notions: Tapestry needle
Gauge: 18 sts and 36 rows = 4" / 10cm in garter stitch

Pattern Notes: (k1, yfwd, k1) into next st - You will work a knit stitch without slipping yarn off the left needle. Then, wrap yarn around the needle as you would for a yarn over, work another knit stitch into that same stitch. Finally, you can slip the stitch off the left needle. You just created 3 stitches from that 1 stitch.

INSTRUCTIONS

Using US 7 / 4.5mm needles, CO 88 sts. The brim is worked back and forth in garter stitch.

Next Row (WS): K all sts.

Next Row (RS): K56, w&t.

Next Row (WS): K24, w&t.

Next 2 Rows: K to end of row, knitting wrap together with wrapped stitch.

Next Row (RS): K60, w&t.

Next Row (WS): K32, w&t.

Next 2 Rows: K to end of row, knitting wrap together with wrapped stitch.

Next Row (RS): K64, w&t.

Next Row (WS): K40, w&t.

Next 2 Rows: K to end of row, knitting wrap together with wrapped stitch.

Next Row (RS): K68, w&t.

Next Row (WS): K48, w&t.

Next 2 Rows: K to end of row, knitting wrap together with wrapped stitch.

Next Row (RS): K72, w&t.

Next Row (WS): K56, w&t.

Next 2 Rows: K to end of row, knitting wrap together with wrapped stitch.

Next Row (RS): K76, w&t.

Next Row (WS): K64, w&t.

Next 2 Rows: K to end of row, knitting wrap together with wrapped stitch.

Next Row (RS): K80, w&t.

Next Row (WS): K72, w&t.

Next 2 Rows: K to end of row, knitting wrap together with wrapped stitch.

Next Row (RS): K84, w&t.

Next Row (WS): K80, w&t.

Next 2 Rows: K to end of row, knitting wrap together with wrapped stitch.

Next Row (RS): (K10, kfb) 8 times. 96 sts.

Place marker and join to work in the rnd.

Rnd 1: K1, *k3, (k1, yfwd, k1) into next st, k1, (turn to WS, p5, turn to RS, k5) twice, k1, repeat from * to last 5 sts, k3, (k1, yfwd, k1) into next st, k1, (turn to WS, p5, turn to RS, k5) twice.

Rnd 2: (K3, ssk, k1, k2tog) to end of rnd.

Rnd 3: *K1, (k1, yfwd, k1) into next st, k1, (turn to WS, p5, turn to RS, k5) twice, k3, repeat from * to end of rnd.

Rnd 4: (Ssk, k1, k2tog, k3) to end of rnd.

Repeat last 4 rnds twice more or until work measures approximately 5.5" / 14cm, ending with Rnd 4.

CROWN SHAPING

Rnd 1: **Ssk, k1, *k1, (k1, yfwd, k1) into next st, k1, (turn to WS, p5, turn to RS, k5) twice, k3, repeat from * twice more, k1, k2tog, repeat from ** 3 more times. 88 sts.

Rnd 2: *K2, (ssk, k1, k2tog, k3) 3 times, k2, repeat from * 3 more times.

Rnd 3: **Ssk, *k4, (k1, yfwd, k1) into next st, k1, (turn to WS, p5, turn to RS, k5) twice, repeat from * twice more, k2tog, repeat from ** 3 more times. 80 sts.

Rnd 4: *K1, (k3, ssk, k1, k2tog) 3 times, k1, repeat from * 3 more times.

Rnd 5: **Ssk, k2, *k4, (k1, yfwd, k1) into next st, k1, (turn to WS, p5, turn to RS, k5) twice, repeat from * once more, k2, k2tog, repeat from ** 3 more times. 72 sts.

Rnd 6: *K3, (k3, ssk, k1, k2tog) 2 times, k3, repeat from * 3 more times.

Rnd 7: **Ssk, k1, *k1, (k1, yfwd, k1) into next st, k1, (turn to WS, p5, turn to RS, k5) twice, k3, repeat from * once more, k1, k2tog, repeat from *8 3 more times. 64 sts.

Rnd 8: *K2, (ssk, k1, k2tog, k3) twice, k2, repeat from * 3 more times.

Rnd 9: **Ssk, *k4, (k1, yfwd, k1) into next st, k1, (turn to WS, p5, turn to RS, k5) twice, repeat from * once more, k2tog. 56 sts.

Rnd 10: *K1, (k3, ssk, k1, k2tog) twice, k1, repeat from * 3 more times.

Rnd 11: *Ssk, k2, k4, (k1, yfwd, k1) into next st, k1, (turn to WS, p5, turn to RS, k5) twice, k2, k2tog, repeat from * 3 more times. 48 sts.

Rnd 12: *K6, ssk, k1, k2tog, k3, repeat from * 3 more times.

Rnd 13: *Ssk, k2, (k1, yfwd, k1) into next st, k1, (turn to WS, p5, turn to RS, k5) twice, k4, k2tog, repeat from * 3 more times. 40 sts.

Rnd 14: *Ssk twice, k1, k2tog, k3, k2tog, repeat from * 3 more times. 32 sts.

Rnd 15: *Ssk, k4, k2tog, repeat from * 3 more times. 24 sts.

Rnd 16: *Ssk, k2, k2tog, repeat from * 3 more times. 16 sts.

Rnd 17: *Ssk, k2tog, repeat from * 3 more times. 8 sts.

FINISHING

Break yarn and pull strand through remaining 8 sts. Sew the garter stitch brim closed. Weave in ends.

THENDARA

I don't think anyone can have too many shawls so I returned to one of my favorite construction methods to whip up this graphic top-down design. Two colors are worked with increases to form a triangle and then two additional locations of increases are added, which transform the shape into a unique piece of architectural knitting. The extra fabric formed by the increases causes the shawl to drape beautifully whether it is resting across the shoulders or tossed around the neck.

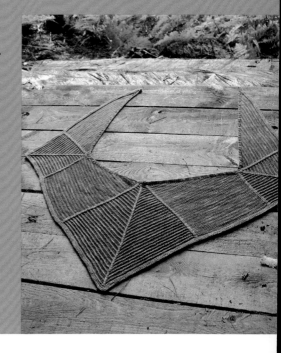

Finished Measurements: 15.5" / 39cm from CO to BO along center stitch, 58" / 147cm wingspan along top edge stitches. Measurements taken after blocking.
Yarn: Sport weight
Yardage: Color A: 270yds / 247m, Color B: 210yds / 192m
Shown in: Madelinetosh Pashmina (75% Merino, 15% Silk, 10% Cashmere; 360yds / 329m per 120g skein), Color A: Wren, Color B: Boxwood
Needles: 32" US 4 / 3.5mm circular
Gauge: 24 sts and 36 rows = 4" / 10cm in stockinette stitch

Pattern Notes: Slipped sts are slipped wyib on the RS. Slipped sts are slipped wyif on the WS. The tendency is for the right edge to be tight where the color change takes place. Carry yarns loosely along that right edge when striping so that there is enough stretch to allow for blocking. Repeat Rows 1-4 of Section 2 for a larger shawl.

INSTRUCTIONS

SECTION 1

Using color A, CO 3 sts. K8 rows.

At the end of last row, do not turn to work other side, rotate piece 90 degrees clockwise so that you are looking at the long side of the garter rectangle. Pick up and k4 sts (in the purl bump of each garter ridge). Rotate piece another 90 degrees. Pick up and k3 sts along the CO edge. Turn to work WS row.

Next Row (WS): K3, yo, p4, yo, k3. 12 sts.

Next Row (RS): K3, yo, k6, yo, k3. 14 sts.

Next Row (WS): K3, yo, p8, yo, k3. 16 sts.

Next Row (RS): Using color B, k3, yo, k2, pm, sl2,

M1R, pm, sl2, pm, M1L, sl2, pm, k2, yo, k3. 20 sts.

Next Row (WS): K3, yo, p to m, slm, sl2, p1, slm, sl2, slm, p1, sl2, slm, p to last 3 sts, yo, k3. 22 sts.

Row 1 (RS): Using color A, k3, yo, k to m, slm, k to m, M1R, slm, k2, slm, M1L, k to m, slm, k to last 3 sts, yo, k3.

Row 2 (WS): K3, yo, p to m, slm, sl2, k to m, slm, p2, slm, k to 2 sts before m, p2, slm, p to last 3 sts, yo, k3.

Row 3 (RS): Using color B, k3, yo, k to m, slm, sl2, k to m, M1R, slm, sl2, slm, M1L, k to 2 sts before m, sl2, slm, k to last 3 sts, yo, k3.

Row 4 (WS): K3, yo, p to m, slm, sl2, p to m, slm, sl2, slm, p to 2 sts before m, sl2, slm, p to last 3 sts, yo, k3.

Repeat last 4 rows until work measures about 5" / 13cm from CO edge (measured along center column of slipped sts), ending with Row 4 (WS). Break color B.

SECTION 2

Next Row (RS): Using color A, K3, yo, k2, w&t.

Next Row (WS): P3, yo, k3.

Repeat last 2 rows twice more.

Next Row (RS): K3, yo, k to m (knitting wraps together with wrapped sts), slm, k to m, M1R, slm, k2, slm, M1L, k to m, slm, k to last 3 sts, yo, k3.

Next Row (WS): K3, yo, p2, w&t.

Next Row (RS): K3, yo, k3.

Repeat last 2 rows twice more.

Next Row (WS): K3, yo, p to m (purling wraps together with wrapped sts), slm, p2, k to m, slm, p2, slm, k to 2 sts before m, p2, slm, p to last 3 sts, yo, k3.

Next Row (RS): Using color B, k3, yo, k4, *pm, sl2, M1R, pm, sl2, pm, M1L, sl2, pm,* k to m, slm, sl2, k to m, M1R, slm, sl2, slm, M1L, k to last 13 sts, repeat from * to *, k4, yo, k3.

Next Row (WS): K3, yo, (p to m, slm, sl2, p to m, slm, sl2, slm, p to 2 sts before m, sl2, slm) 3 times, p to last 3 sts, yo, k3.

Row 1 (RS): Using color A, k3, yo, (k to m, slm, k to m, M1R, slm, k2, slm, M1L, k to m, slm) 3 times, k to last 3 sts, yo, k3.

Row 2 (WS): K3, yo, (p to m, slm, p2, k to m, slm, p2, slm, k to 2 sts before m, p2, slm) 3 times, p to last 3 sts, yo, k3.

Row 3 (RS): Using color B, k3, yo, (k to m, slm, sl2, k to m, M1R, slm, sl2, slm, M1L, k to 2 sts before m, sl2, slm) 3 times, k to last 3 sts, yo, k3.

Row 4 (WS): K3, yo, (p to m, slm, sl2, p to m, slm, sl2, slm, p to 2 sts before m, sl2, slm) 3 times, p to last 3 sts, yo, k3.

Repeat last 4 rows until work measures about 14" / 36cm from CO edge (measured along center column of slipped sts), ending with Row 4 (WS). Break color B. Rows 1-4 can easily be repeated for a larger shawl.

SECTION 3

Row 1 (RS): Using color A, k3, yo, (k to m, slm, k to m, M1R, slm, k2, slm, M1L, k to m, slm) 3 times, k to last 3 sts, yo, k3.

Row 2 (WS): K3, yo, k to last 3 sts, yo, k3.

Repeat last 2 rows twice more.

FINISHING

BO all sts on following RS row as follows, (k2tog tbl, slip st back to left needle) to end of row. Break yarn, weave in ends, and block to desired dimensions.

WEDGEWOOD

Garter and stockinette stitch are featured in this fingering weight length-wise scarf, made to show off a pair of beautiful yarns. Short row shaping in the stockinette section creates long wedges, perfect for colorful variegated or self-striping yarns. Three I-cord buttonholes with toggles add to the many different ways of wearing this scarf.

Finished Measurements: 70" / 178cm long, 13" / 33cm wide at widest point. Measurements taken after blocking.
Yarn: Fingering weight, Color A: 420 yds / 384m, Color B: 200 yds / 183m
Shown in: Color A - Hedgehog Fibres Yak Yarn (75% Yak Down, 25% Bamboo; 383yds / 350m per 100g skein); Color B - Hedgehog Fibres Sock Yarn (85% Superwash Merino, 15% Nylon; 383yds / 350m per 100g skein), Colorway: Winter Thaw
Needles: 32" US 4 / 3.5mm circular
Notions: 4 stitch markers, tapestry needle, three 1-inch toggles or buttons
Gauge: 22 sts and 40 rows = 4" / 10cm in garter stitch

Pattern Notes: In Rows 1-10, the 1st stitch marker refers to the one closest to the right edge with RS facing, so the last stitch marker is the one closest to the left edge with RS facing.

INSTRUCTIONS

SECTION 1
Using color A, CO 306 sts.

Next Row (WS): K87, pm, (k70, pm) 3 times, k5, sl4 wyif. 4 stitch markers placed.

Repeat last row 14 more times, ending with a WS row. There should be 8 garter ridges.

Next Row (RS): Using color A, k16, using color B, k to 1 st before last m, w&t.

Skip Row 1 (RS) and continue by working Row 2 (WS).

**Row 1 (RS): Using color A, k16, xAB, using color B, k to 1 st before last m, w&t.

Row 2 (WS): P to last 16 sts, xBA, using color A, k12, sl4 wyif.

Row 3 (RS): K16, xAB, using color B, k to 1 st before 3rd m, w&t.

Row 4 (WS): P to last 16 sts, xBA, using color A, k12, sl4 wyif.

Row 5 (RS): K16, xAB, using color B, k to 1 st before 2nd m, w&t.

Row 6 (WS): P to last 16 sts, xBA, using color A, k12, sl4 wyif.

Row 7 (RS): K16, xAB, using color B, k to 1 st before 1st m, w&t.

Row 8 (WS): P to last 16 sts, xBA, using color A, k12, sl4 wyif.

Row 9 (RS): Using color A, k to last 4 sts (knitting wraps together with wrapped stitches), sl4 wyif.

Row 10 (WS): K to last 4 sts, sl4 wyif.

Repeat last row twice more, ending with a WS row.

Repeat from ** 7 more times, resulting in 8 color B wedges. Break color B.

Continue repeating Row 10 twelve more times, ending with a WS row. There should be 8 garter ridges.

FINISHING

BO all sts loosely on following RS row as follows, (k2tog tbl, slip stitch back to left needle) to end of row. Break yarn and work 3 I-cord buttonholes evenly across the skinnier end of the scarf.

I-cord buttonholes: Pick up and k4 sts on the WS of I-cord edge (at skinnier end of the scarf). (K4, sl4 sts back to left needle) 10 times or until I-cord is desired length. Break yarn and pull it through the 4 sts. Sew I-cord down to WS of fabric to form a loop.

Weave in ends and block lightly to smooth fabric. Then, sew 3 buttons as pictured. Button placement can vary so try the scarf on to gauge where you would like the buttons to go.

OLD FORGE

This big blanket is worked from the center outward in a cozy worsted weight wool. The bold colorwork sun transitions into simple lace followed by a knit/purl chevron pattern, and finally finishes with an attached garter stitch edge. Old Forge is sure to keep your lap warm while you eagerly knit each section. Try working with a fingering weight yarn for a lighter shawl/wrap.

Finished Measurements: 65" / 165cm diameter. Measurements taken after blocking.
Yarn: Worsted weight
Shown in: Color A - Beaverslide Dry Goods Merino/Mohair (90% Merino, 10% Mohair; 241yds/ 226m per 113g skein), Colorway: Autumn Haze
Color B - Beaverslide Dry Goods Natural Heather (100% Merino; 241yds / 226m per 113g skein), Colorway: Natural Heather
Yardage: Color A - 285yds / 261m
Color B - 1,850yds / 1,692m
Needles: 1 set US 10 / 6mm DPNS
60" US 10 / 6mm circular
6mm (J) crochet hook for CO
Notions: 5 stitch markers, tapestry needle
Gauge: 16 sts and 22 rows = 4" / 10 cm in stockinette stitch

Pattern Notes: Stitches are slipped wyib. m1: (make one) increase one stitch by knitting into the stitch below
Reading the Charts: Charted rnds are read from right to left starting at the bottom.

INSTRUCTIONS

Using color A and DPNs, CO 8 sts. I used Emily Ocker's circular CO method. Distribute sts evenly onto 4 DPNs. Place marker and join to work in the rnd. Switch to circular needles when there are too many sts to fit onto DPNs.

SECTION 1

Rnd 1: K8.

Rnd 2: (M1, k1) 8 times. 16 sts.

Rnd 3: K16.

Rnd 4: (M1, k1) 16 times. 32 sts.

Next 4 rnds: K all sts.

Rnd 9: (M1, k1) 32 times. 64 sts.

Next 10 rnds: K all sts.

Rnd 20: (M1, k1) 64 times. 128 sts.

SECTION 2

Rnds 1 & 2: Using color A, k all sts.

Rnd 3: Using color B, (k6, sl2) 16 times.

Rnd 4: (P6, sl2) 16 times.

Repeat last 4 rnds 5 more times.

Rnd 25: Using color A, k all sts.

Rnd 26: *(M1, k1) 6 times, k2, repeat from * 15 more times. 224 sts.

Rnd 27: Using color B, (k12, sl2) 16 times.

Rnd 28: (P12, sl2) 16 times.

Rnds 29 & 30: Using color A, k all sts.

Rnd 31: Using color B, (k12, sl2) 16 times.

Rnd 32: (P12, sl2) 16 times.

Rnds 33 & 34: Using color A, k all sts.

Rnd 35: Using color B, (k26, sl2) 8 times.

Rnd 36: (P26, sl2) 8 times.

SECTION 4

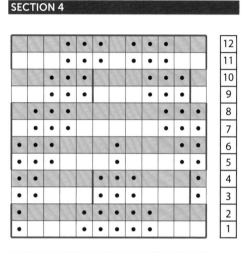

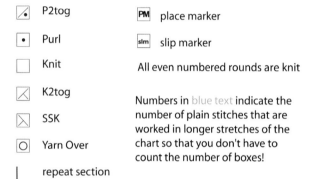

	P2tog
•	Purl
	Knit
	K2tog
	SSK
O	Yarn Over
│	repeat section

PM place marker

slm slip marker

All even numbered rounds are knit

Numbers in blue text indicate the number of plain stitches that are worked in longer stretches of the chart so that you don't have to count the number of boxes!

SECTION 3

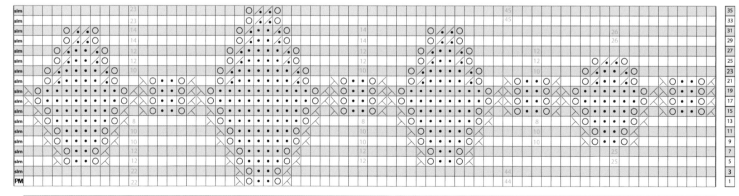

Repeat last 4 rnds 5 more times.

Rnd 57: Using color A, k all sts.

Rnd 58: *(M1, k2) 12 times, (m1, k1) twice, k2 repeat from * 7 more times. 336 sts.

Rnd 59: Using color B, (k40, sl2) 8 times.

Rnd 60: (P40, sl2) 8 times

Rnds 61 & 62: Using color A, k all sts.

Rnd 63: Using color B, (k40, sl2) 8 times.

Rnd 64: (P40, sl2) 8 times.

Rnds 65 & 66: Using color A, k all sts.

Rnd 67: Using color B, k all sts.

Rnd 68: P all sts.

Break color A.

Rnd 69: Using color B, k all sts.

Rnd 70: (M1, k14) 24 times. 360 sts.

Continue by following written or charted instructions. Rnds 1-35 are charted in **SECTION 3**. Only odd numbered rnds are charted. All even numbered rnds are knit.

SECTION 3

Rnds 1 & 3: (K44, k2tog, yo, p2, yo, ssk, k22, pm) 5 times.

All even numbered rnds: K all sts.

Rnd 5 & 7: (K25, k2tog, yo, p2, yo ssk, k12, k2tog, yo, p4, yo, ssk, k12, k2tog, yo, p2, yo, ssk, k3, slm) 5 times.

Rnd 9 & 11: (K8, k2tog, yo, p2, yo ssk, k10, k2tog, yo, p4, yo, ssk, k10, k2tog, yo, p6, yo, ssk, k10, k2tog, yo, p4, yo, ssk, k2, slm) 5 times.

Rnd 13: (K7, k2tog, yo, p4, yo ssk, k8, k2tog, yo, p6, yo, ssk, k8, k2tog, yo, p8, yo, ssk, k8, k2tog, yo, p6, yo, ssk, k1, slm) 5 times.

Rnd 15: (K2tog, yo, p2, yo, ssk, k1, k2tog, yo, p4, yo, ssk, k1, k2tog, yo, p2, yo, ssk, k1, k2tog, yo, p6, yo, ssk, k1, k2tog, yo, p2, yo, ssk, k1, k2tog, yo, p8, yo, ssk, k1, k2tog, yo, p2, yo, ssk, k1, k2tog, yo, p6, yo, ssk, k1, slm) 5 times.

Rnd 17 & 19: (K2tog, yo, p2, yo, ssk, k2tog, yo, p6, yo ssk, k2tog, yo, p2, yo, ssk, k2tog, yo, p8, yo, ssk, k2tog, yo, p2, yo, ssk, k2tog, yo, p10, yo, ssk, k2tog, yo, p2, yo, ssk, k2tog, yo, p8, yo, ssk, slm) 5 times.

Rnd 21: (K2tog, yo, p2, yo, ssk, k2, yo, p2tog p2, p2tog, yo, k2, k2tog, yo, p2, yo, ssk, k2, yo, p2tog, p4, p2tog, yo, k2, k2tog, yo, p2, yo, ssk, k2, yo, p2tog, p6, p2tog, yo, k2, k2tog, yo, p2, yo, ssk, k2, yo, p2tog, p4, p2tog, yo, k2, slm) 5 times.

Rnd 23: (K8, yo, p2tog, p2, p2tog, yo, k10, yo, p2tog, p4, p2tog, yo, k10, yo, p2tog, p6, p2tog, yo, k10, yo, p2tog, p4, p2tog, yo, k2, slm) 5 times.

Rnd 25 & 27: (K9, yo, p2tog twice, yo, k12, yo, p2tog, p2, p2tog, yo, k12, yo, p2tog, p4, p2tog, yo, k12, yo, p2tog, p2, p2tog, yo, k3, slm) 5 times.

Rnd 29 & 31: (K26, yo, p2tog twice, yo, k14, yo, p2tog, p2, p2tog, yo, k14, yo, p2tog twice, yo, k4, slm) 5 times.

Rnd 33 & 35: (K45, yo, p2tog twice, yo, k23, slm) 5 times.

Rnd 36: K all sts.

Rnd 37: *(M1, k1) twice, k1, repeat from * to end of rnd. 600 sts.

Rnd 38: P all sts.

Rnd 39: K all sts.

Continue by following written or charted instructions for **SECTION 4**. Rnds 1-12 are charted and those 12 rnds are repeated twice.

SECTION 4

Rnds 1 & 2: (K3, p5, k3, p1) to end of rnd.

Rnd 3 & 4: P1, (k3, p3) to last 5 sts, k3, p2.

Rnd 5 & 6: (P2, k3, p1, k3, p3) to end of rnd.

Rnd 7 & 8: (P3, k5, p3, k1) to end of rnd.

Rnd 9 & 10: K1, (p3, k3) to last 5 sts, p3, k2.

Rnd 11 & 12: (K2, p3, k1, p3, k3) to end of rnd.

Repeat last 12 rnds twice more.

Rnd 37: K all sts.

Rnd 38: P all sts.

Rnd 39: K all sts.

BORDER

The garter stitch border is worked back and forth and attached as it is being worked.

Using the cabled CO method, CO 10 sts.

Row 1 (RS): K9, k2tog.

Row 2 (WS): K9, sl1 wyif.

Repeat last 2 rows until all 600 sts have been worked together with garter stitch border.

FINISHING

BO all sts on following RS row. Sew BO edge to CO edge. Break yarn and weave in ends. Block blanket to desired measurements.

DUSTLAND HAT

This textured hat gives the perfect amount of slouch for a cozy casual look. The knit-purl patterning beautifully highlights a solid worsted weight yarn. An optional button can be added to tack down the slouchy fabric.

Sizes: Small [Medium, Large]
Finished Measurements: 19 [21, 22.5]" / 48 [53, 57]cm. Hats are shown on a 22.5" / 57cm head.
Yarn: Worsted weight
Yardage: 160 [180, 200]yds / 146 [165, 183]m
Shown in: Small Dark Version – Elsa Wool Company Woolen-Spun Worsted Weight Cormo (100% Wool; 238yds / 218m per 113g skein), Colorway: Dark Grey
Medium Light Version - Swans Island Certified Organic Merino Worsted (100% Merino; 250yds/ 229m per 100g skein), Colorway: Grey
Needles: 16" US 6 / 4mm circular
16" US 7 / 4.5mm circular
1 set of US 7 / 4.5mm DPNs
Notions: 1 stitch marker, tapestry needle, 1" button (optional)
Gauge: 20 sts = 4" / 10cm in garter stitch

INSTRUCTIONS

Using US 6/ 4mm needles, CO 88 [96. 104] sts. Place marker and join to work in the rnd, being careful not to twist sts.

2 x 2 ribbing: (K2, p2) to end of rnd.

Repeat 2 x 2 ribbing until work measures 1.5" / 4cm from CO edge. Switch to US 7 / 4.5mm needles.

K 1 rnd.
P 1 rnd.

Repeat last 2 rnds once more.

K 1 rnd.

SECTION 1

Rnd 1: (K2, p2) to end of rnd.

Rnd 2: K1, (p2, k2) to 3 sts before end of rnd, p2, k1.

Rnd 3: (P2, k2) to end of rnd.

Rnd 4: P1, (k2, p2) to 3 sts before end of rnd, k2, p1.

Repeat last 4 rnds once more.

Next Rnd: (K10 [11, 12], kfb) 8 times. 96 [104, 112] sts.

P 1 rnd.
K 1 rnd.

Repeat last 2 rnds once more.

SECTION 2

Rnds 1 & 2: (K1, p1) to end of rnd.

Rnd 3 & 4: (P1, k1) to end of rnd.

Repeat last 4 rnds once more.

K 1 rnd.

P 1 rnd.
K 1 rnd.

Repeat last 2 rnds once more.

SECTION 3

Rnd 1: (K2, p2) to end of rnd.

Rnd 2: K to end of rnd.

Repeat last 2 rnds 3 more times.

P 1 rnd.

K 1 rnd.

Repeat last 2 rnds once more.

SECTION 4

Rnd 1: (K2, p2) to end of rnd.

Rnd 2: K1, (p2, k2) to 3 sts before end of rnd, p2, k1.

Rnd 3: (P2, k2) to end of rnd.

Rnd 4: P1, (k2, p2) to 3 sts before end of rnd, k2, p1.

Repeat last 4 rnds once more.

K 1 rnd.

P 1 rnd.

Repeat last 2 rnds once more.

CROWN SHAPING

Next Rnd: (K12 [11, 5], k0 [k2tog, k2tog]) 8 [8, 16] times. 96 sts. 0 [8, 16] sts decreased.

Rnds 1 & 2: (K1, p1) to end of rnd.

Rnd 3 & 4: (P1, k1) to end of rnd.

Repeat last 4 rnds once more.

Rnd 9: (K4, k2tog) 16 times. 80 sts.

P 1 rnd.

K 1 rnd.

Repeat last 2 rnds once more.

Rnd 14: (K2, p2) to end of rnd.

Rnd 15: K all sts.

Repeat last 2 rnds once more.

Rnd 18: (K2, p2tog) to end of rnd. 60 sts.

Rnd 19: K all sts.

Rnd 20: (K2, p1) to end of rnd.

Rnd 21: (K1, ssk) to end of rnd. 40 sts.

P 1 rnd.

K 1 rnd.

Repeat last 2 rnds once more.

Rnd 26: P2tog to end of rnd. 20 sts.

Rnd 27: K all sts.

Rnd 28: P2tog to end of rnd. 10 sts.

FINISHING

Break yarn and pull through remaining sts. Weave in ends and block hat to smooth the fabric. Optional - Sew a button onto the back of the hat to tack down the slouchy fabric.

DUSTLAND MITTS

These casual fingerless mitts are easy to knit, but changes in the patterning keep you engaged. Fingering weight yarn gives these comfy mitts the perfect amount of slouch and warmth. They're great for biking around town or working on the computer.

Finished Measurements: 8" / 20cm circumference, 13" / 33cm long
Yarn: Fingering weight
Yardage: 210yds / 192m
Shown in: Blue Green version - Shilasdair Fingering (20% Cashmere, 40% Angora, 40% Lambswool; 220yds / 200m per 50g skein) Colorway: Juniper
Natural version – Beaverslide Dry Goods 2 ply Sport/Sock Weight (80% Merino, 20% Mohair; 458yds / 419m per 113g skein) Colorway: Natural Buff
Needles: 1 set US 4 / 3.5mm DPNs
Notions: 1 stitch marker, tapestry needle
Gauge: 22 sts = 4" / 10cm in garter stitch

Pattern Notes: One size is provided, but you can choose a smaller needle for a smaller mitt circumference.

INSTRUCTIONS

CO 48 sts and divide sts evenly onto DPNs. Place marker and join to work in the rnd, being careful not to twist sts.

2 x 2 ribbing: (K2, p2) to end of rnd.

Repeat 2 x 2 ribbing until work measures 1.5" / 4cm from CO edge.

K 1 rnd.
P 1 rnd.

Repeat last 2 rnds once more.

K 1 rnd.

SECTION 1

Rnd 1: (K2, p2) to end of rnd.

Rnd 2: K1, (p2, k2) to 3 sts before end of rnd, p2, k1.

Rnd 3: (P2, k2) to end of rnd.

Rnd 4: P1, (k2, p2) to 3 sts before end of rnd, k2, p1.

Repeat last 4 rnds once more.

K 1 rnd.

P 1 rnd.
K 1 rnd.

Repeat last 2 rnds once more.

SECTION 2

Rnds 1 & 2: (K1, p1) to end of rnd.

Rnd 3 & 4: (P1, k1) to end of rnd.

Repeat last 4 rnds once more.

K 1 rnd.

P 1 rnd.
K 1 rnd.

Repeat last 2 rnds once more.

SECTION 3

Rnd 1: (K2, p2) to end of rnd.

Rnd 2: K to end of rnd.

Repeat last 2 rnds 3 more times.

P 1 rnd.

K 1 rnd.

Repeat last 2 rnds once more.

Repeat Sections 1-3 once more.

RIGHT THUMB GUSSET

Rnd 1: (K2, p2) 9 times. pm, M1R, k2, p2, M1L, pm, (k2, p2) twice.

Rnd 2: K1, (p2, k2) 8 times, p2, k1, slm, p1, k2, p2, k1, slm, k1, p2, k2, p2, k1.

Rnd 3: (P2, k2) 9 times, slm, M1R, p1, k2, p2, k1, M1L, slm, (p2, k2) twice.

Rnd 4: P1, (k2, p2) 8 times, k2, p1, slm, (p2, k2) twice, slm, p1, k2, p2, k2, p1.

Rnd 5: (K2, p2) 9 times. slm, M1R, (p2, k2) twice, M1L, slm, (p2, k2) twice.

Rnd 6: K1, (p2, k2) 8 times, p2, k1, slm, k1, (p2, k2) twice, p1 slm, k1, p2, k2, p2, k1.

Rnd 7: (P2, k2) 9 times, slm, M1R, k1, (p2, k2) twice, p1, M1L, slm, (p2, k2) twice.

Rnd 8: P1, (k2, p2) 8 times, k2, p1, slm, (p2, k2) 3 times, slm, p1, k2, p2, k2, p1.

Rnd 9: K to m, slm, M1R, (p2, k2) 3 times, M1L, slm, k to end of rnd.

Rnd 10: P to m, slm, p1, (k2, p2) 3 times, k1, slm, p to end of rnd.

Rnd 11: K to m, slm, M1R, p1, (k2, p2) 3 times, k1, M1L, slm, k to end of rnd.

Rnd 12: P to m, sl16 gusset sts to scrap yarn, CO 4 sts, p to end of rnd.

Rnd 13: K to end of rnd.

LEFT THUMB GUSSET

Rnd 1: (K2, p2) twice, pm, M1R, k2, p2, M1L, pm, (k2, p2) 9 times.

Rnd 2: K1, p2, k2, p2, k1, slm, p1, k2, p2, k1, slm, k1, (p2, k2) 8 times, p2, k1.

Rnd 3: (P2, k2) twice, slm, M1R, p1, k2, p2, k1, M1L, slm, (p2, k2) 9 times.

Rnd 4: P1, k2, p2, k2, p1, slm, (p2, k2) twice, slm, p1, (k2, p2) 8 times, k2, p1.

Rnd 5: (K2, p2) twice, slm, M1R, (p2, k2) twice, M1L, slm, (k2, p2) 9 times.

Rnd 6: K1, p2, k2, p2, k1, slm, k1, (p2, k2) twice, p1 slm, k1, (p2, k2) 8 times, p2, k1.

Rnd 7: (P2, k2) twice, slm, M1R, k1, (p2, k2) twice, p1, M1L, slm, (p2, k2) 9 times.

Rnd 8: P1, k2, p2, k2, p1, slm, (p2, k2) 3 times, slm, p1, (k2, p2) 8 times, k2, p1.

Rnd 9: K to m, slm, M1R, (k2, p2) 3 times, M1L, slm, k to end of rnd.

Rnd 10: P to m, slm, p1, (k2, p2) 3 times, k1, slm, p to end of rnd.

Rnd 11: K to m, slm, M1R, p1, (k2, p2) 3 times, k1, M1L, slm, k to end of rnd.

Rnd 12: P to m, sl16 gusset sts to scrap yarn, CO 4 sts, p to end of rnd.

Rnd 13: K to end of rnd.

BOTH MITTS CONT.

Repeat SECTION 2 once more, then work 1.5" / 4cm of 2 x 2 ribbing.

BO all sts on next rnd.

THUMBS

Place 16 sts from thumb gusset onto DPNs.

Set Up Rnd: (P2, k2) 4 times, pick up and k4 sts where sts were CO during the thumb gusset shaping. Place marker and join to work in the rnd.

Next 10 Rnds: (P2, k2) 5 times.

FINISHING

BO all sts. Break yarn and weave in ends.

Join

the Westknits Fan Club

for news, updates,

pattern support,

and friendship!

www.ravelry.com/groups/westknits-fan-club

"Westknits offered me a whole
new perspective on knitting!"
– Nicolás (Argentina)

"Thanks to the Westknits Fan
Club, I can feel my power as
a woman, and I learned how
to channel my energies into a
creative goal!"
– Clara (Switzerland/Brazil)

"Through the Westknits fan club
I realized knitting is actually
cool and very up to date."
– Louis (Belgium)

TERHI MONTONEN (mustaavillaa)
Lohja, Finland
Longview
Yarn: Orange Flower Twist HW

MARGARITA LAUTIER (1funkyknitwit)
Sydney, Australia
Bedrock
Yarn: Hand-Dyed Handspun
Modifications: 2 full pattern repeats before crown shaping

Dustland Mitts
Yarn: Knitabulous – FiftyFifty

Moose River
Yarn: Cascade 220

ANNE (anneleterme)
South West France
Dustland Hat
Yarn: Holst Garn Supersoft 100% uld

Dustland Mitts
Yarn: Holst Garn Supersoft 100% uld

Bedrock
Yarn: Manos del Uruguay Wool Clasica

Bedrock
Yarn: Fyperspates Scrumptious Solid DK

BETH ABRILES (tangobka)
Madison, Connecticut, USA
Dustland Hat
Yarn: Quince & Co Chickadee

Seaway
Yarn: Sundara Worsted Merino

VERONICA MOELLER (VeronicaMM)
Pearland, Texas, USA
Dustland Hat
Yarn: Madelinetosh Tosh DK

Dustland Mitts
Yarn: Madelinetosh Tosh Sock

Longview
Yarn: Plymouth Yarn Baby Alpaca Grande

Wedgewood
Yarn: Knit it Up Squishy
Modifications: 5 short row wedges

WILL GILLESPIE (willyg)
Southern New Jersey, USA
Dustland Hat
Yarn: Llamajama Alpaca Merino Wool

SUSANNE SINDEVSKI (KnitaholicSusanne)
Woolongong, Australia
Wedgewood
Yarn: Old Maiden Aunt Merino Superwash 4ply &
Skein Frog and Toad

Thendara
Yarn: Madelinetosh Tosh Merino Light

HOLLY MCALISTER (Hollisann)
Tulsa, OK, USA
Thendara
Yarn: Ella Rae Lace & Hand-Dyed

(PHOTOS THAT DIDN'T QUITE MAKE IT)

The Sun Satchel doubles as a hat!

Dustland Hat – The perfect accessory for sassy lumberjacks.

Susan's dog ready for her closeup.

I wouldn't let the reporter in Iceland interview me unless he modeled the hat.

Iceland's ocean wind made photographing scarves quite difficult.

ABBREVIATIONS

BO: bind off

C2B for Seaway: (cable 2 back) slip 1 stitch to cable needle and hold in back of work, k1tbl, p1 from cable needle

C2F for Seaway: (cable 2 front) slip 1 stitch to cable needle and hold in front of work, p1, k1tbl from cable needle

C4B for Longview: (cable 4 back) slip 2 stitches to cable needle and hold in back of work, k2, k2 from cable needle

C4F for Longview: (cable 4 front) slip 2 stitches to cable needle and hold in front of work, k2, k2 from cable needle

C4B for Moose River: (cable 4 back) slip 2 stitches to cable needle and hold in back of work, k2, p2 from cable needle

C4F for Moose River: (cable 4 front) slip 2 stitches to cable needle and hold in front of work, p2, k2 from cable needle

C6B: (cable 6 back) slip 3 stitches to cable needle and hold in back of work, k3, k3 from cable needle

C6F: (cable 6 front) slip 3 stitches to cable needle and hold in front of work, k3, k3 from cable needle

C8B: (cable 8 back) slip 4 stitches to cable needle and hold in back of work, k4, k4 from cable needle

C8F: (cable 8 front) slip 4 stitches to cable needle and hold in front of work, k4, k4 from cable needle

CO: cast on

k: knit

k2tog: knit two together

kfb: knit into front and back of stitch

m: marker

m1: (make one) increase one stitch by knitting into the stitch below

M1L: (make one left) with left needle, lift strand between sts from the front, knit through the back loop

M1R: (make one right) with left needle, lift strand between sts from the back, knit through the front loop

p: purl

p2tog: purl two together

p3tog: purl three together

pfb: purl into front and back of stitch

pm: place marker

rnd/s: round/s

RS: right side

sl: slip

slm: slip marker

ssk: slip slip knit

st/s: stitch/es

tbl: through back loop

w&t: (wrap and turn) Bring yarn to front as if you are about to purl, slip one stitch purl-wise. Turn work to other side. Strand of yarn is now in back of work. Bring yarn to the front, slip one stitch back to right needle. Continue to knit or purl the next stitch as instructed.

WS: wrong side

wyib: with yarn in back

wyif: with yarn in front

xAB: cross color A strand over color B

xBA: cross color B strand over color A

yfwd: yarn forward

yo: yarn over

MODEL

Roy Harrington Tracy grew up in a small mountain village in the Adirondack Park. He is a dancer and an artist. He is inspired by natural environments, the animal kingdom and folk music, as well as observing human behavior, and always enjoys a nice glass of wine.